BigTime® Piano

中国乐曲

MUSIC FROM CHINA

Arranged by Nancy and Randall Faber

L 4

This book belongs to: _____

Topic Planning: Yishan Zhao
Production Coordinator: Jon Ophoff
Editor/Researcher: Patrick Bachmann
Translator/Editor: Lin Tian
Design and Illustration: Terpstra Design, Wagner Design
Engraving: Dovetree Productions, Inc.

ISBN 978-1-61677-728-9

A NOTE TO TEACHERS

BigTime Piano Music from China is a colorful, pianistic collection of original Chinese piano compositions for mid to late intermediate students. The pieces were carefully selected for appealing dance-like rhythms, dramatic movement across the keyboard, sonorous use of the pedal, as well as faster tempi with crisp articulations. Keys represented are: A minor, G, D, A, B, B♭, and E♭ major.

The music explores many animals such as the panda, giraffe, peacock, and monkey. Other works feature the exciting Dragon Lantern Dance, the lilting patterns of a Shepherd's Song, and a lighthearted game of Hide and Seek. In this collection:

- **Introductory notes** provide context for the pieces.

- **Performance tips** help interpretation.

- **Think Theory** questions and activities explore harmony, form, and musical patterns.

- **Illustrations/photos** offer musical inspiration.

- **Duet Improvisations** and a **Guided Student Composition** help students create their own "sounds of China."

Helpful Hints:

1. Hands-alone practice is often helpful to focus on fingering and melodic and rhythmic patterns. Pieces may also be broken down into sections for focused learning.

2. Difficult passages may be flagged for special practice. Consider colored pencils to mark these measures as "achievement passages."

3. Two-octave "warm-up scales" are given for many pieces. Encourage students to memorize the scales. The "color blocking" of the fingering will help with scale patterns.

4. In Chinese music, it is especially important to pay close attention to the articulation and dynamics. This will help the music to "dance" with exciting contrasts—for a performance full of vitality.

CONTENTS

Introduction to *The Panda* (pp. 6-7)

The first four pieces in this book are movements from a *suite*—a collection of pieces united by a central theme. In this suite, titled "The Zoo," each movement represents a different animal: the panda, giraffe, peacock, and monkey.

Li Yinghai, who was a composition professor at the China Conservatory of Music, wrote this work in 1985.

THE SOUND OF CHINA

The **pentatonic scale** is a 5-note scale that is common in Chinese music. **Penta** means "five," and **tonic** means "tone." Think, five tones!

This piece uses the **A minor pentatonic scale**. This scale refers back to the **C pentatonic scale** except that instead of *starting* and *ending* on **C**, it *starts* and *ends* on **A**.

- Play each pentatonic scale until it's easy.
  Follow the **fingering** and notice where the **skips** (3rds) occur.

The C Pentatonic Scale

The A Minor Pentatonic Scale

Think Theory: *The Panda* (pp. 6-7)

L.H. motive

Look at **p. 6**. "The Panda" begins with a short
L.H. motive based on the **A minor pentatonic scale**.
(A motive is a short musical idea.)

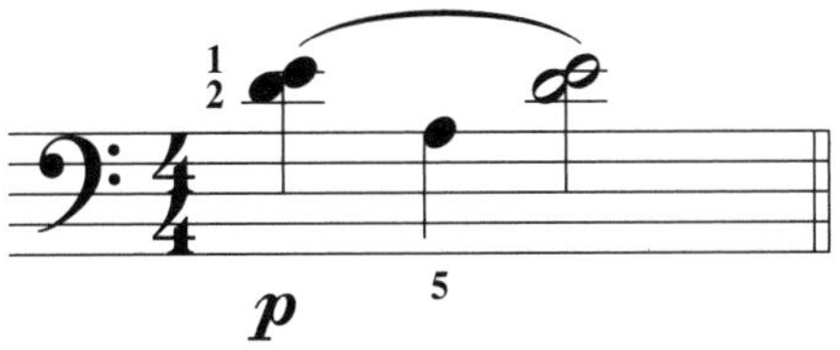

1. Chinese music often features intervals of a **2nd**, **4th**, and **5th**.
   Can you find each of these intervals in the **L.H. motive** shown above?
   Name the notes for each interval.

   2nd: _____ to _____   **4th:** _____ to _____   **5th:** _____ to _____

2. On **p. 6**, where does this **L.H. motive** appear again, now *transposed* down a **5th**?

   measure _____

3. The opening **R.H. theme** at **m. 3** is shown below. Does it use the **A minor pentatonic scale**? (see **p. 4**)

   yes or **no** ? (circle)

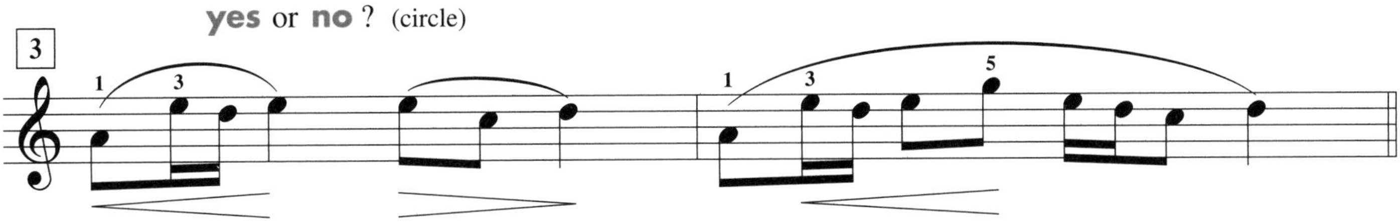

4. Where does the opening **R.H. theme** return later in the piece? (see **pp. 6-7**)

   measure _____

   What *sharp* appears as a "color tone"?

   _____

5. Which **16th-note pattern** is the most commonly used in the piece? (circle)

   or   or

6. On **p. 7**, in **mm. 11-19**, the L.H. plays *one* interval.

   2nd   **3rd**   **4th**   **5th**   (circle)

7. In which *two* measures does the L.H. play **accidentals** that give it an exotic sound?
   (An accidental is a sharp or flat not part of the key signature. A natural is also considered an accidental.)

   measures _____ **and** _____

8. How is the tempo mark *andantino* different than *andante*? (see Music Dictionary, **p. 40**)

   a. It's a little faster than *andante*.   b. It's a little slower than *andante*.

Performance Tips

1. Prepare the **R.H. 5th** before beginning.

2. Let the L.H. wrist rise *slightly* at the end of each motive.

熊 猫
The Panda

Composed by Li Yinghai

Andantino (♩ = 80)

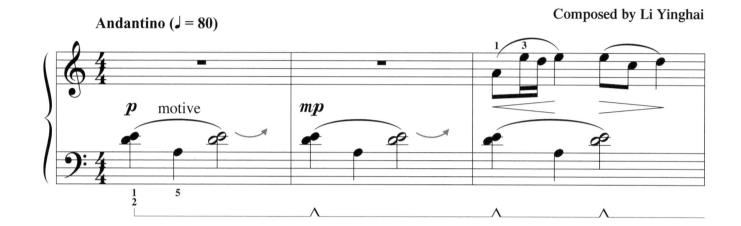
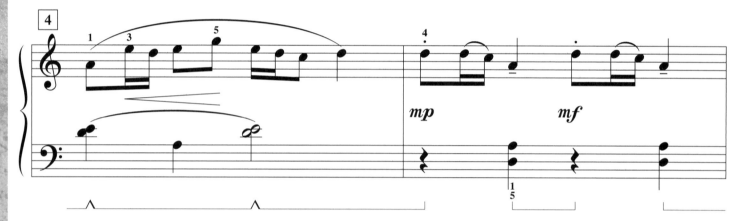
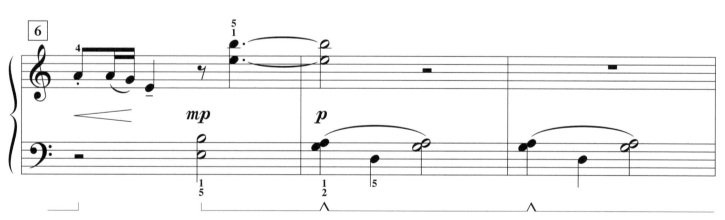
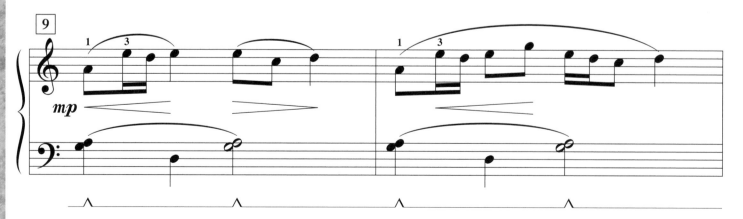

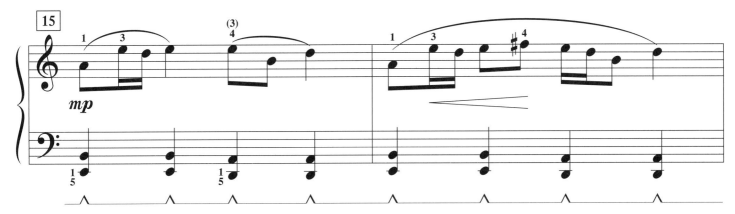

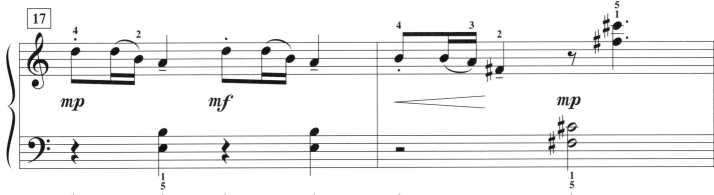

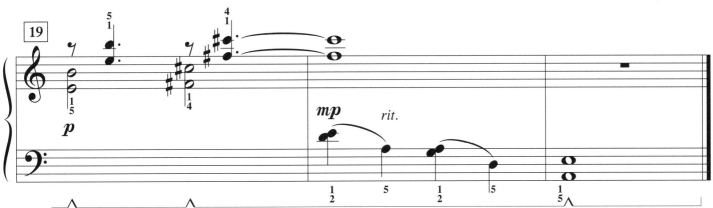

Introduction to *The Giraffe* (pp. 10-11)

The second piece in the suite, "The Giraffe," has an ascending opening melody that stretches over two octaves—tall like a giraffe! Did you know that a giraffe is the tallest mammal on earth?

The giraffe is typically a quiet and graceful animal. The dynamics never reach a *forte* or *fortissimo* in keeping with the giraffe's gentle nature.

Lastly, the giraffe spends most of its life standing up. It even sleeps standing up! For the final two measures, imagine the giraffe standing and sleeping peacefully at night (see p. 11).

Think Theory: *The Giraffe* (pp. 10-11)

1. Turn to **page 10**. Name the **key signature**. _____ **major** or **minor** (circle one) ✏

2. Play and *memorize* the **two-octave D major scale**, hands separately.
   Note: Circled notes indicate *sharp* keys. The highlighted finger numbers will help you see **scale patterns**.

Two-Octave D Major Scale: for R.H.

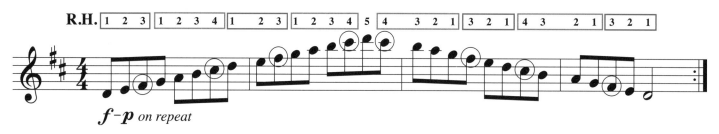

f-p on repeat

Two-Octave D Major Scale: for L.H.

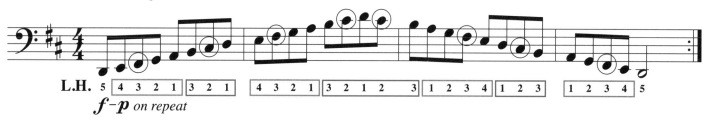

f-p on repeat

3. What does this **time signature** mean?   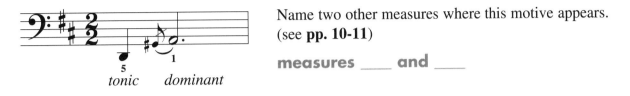 **2** means _____ beats in a measure   ✏

   2 means the _____ note gets one beat

4. In **m. 1**, the L.H. plays the *tonic* (step 1) to the *dominant* (step 5).

   Name two other measures where this motive appears.
   (see **pp. 10-11**)

   measures ____ and ____

   tonic   dominant

5. In **mm. 2-3** (shown below), the "giraffe's neck" stretches from **bass D** to high **treble C♯**.
   Can you analyze what chord is being played? (circle one)

   B minor   D major (add 6)   **G major** (add 6)

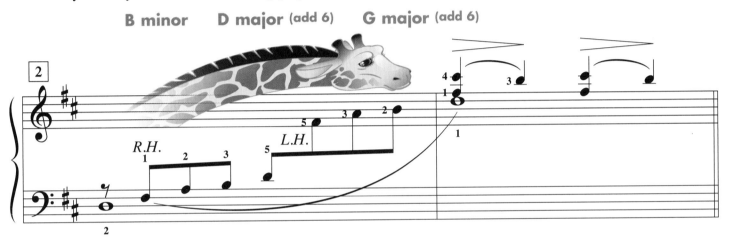

6. Where does **m. 2** (above), return as an *exact* repetition in the piece? **measure _____**

7. In the key of **D major**, **D** is the *tonic* (step 1). **A** is the *dominant* (step 5).
   In **m. 6** (shown below), the R.H. passage floats above **A**, the dominant, in the bass.

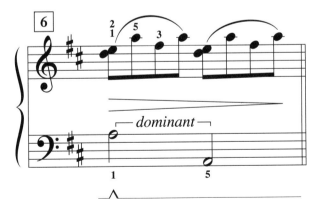

   Look at **p. 11**. Where does the R.H. passage appear again, but this time transposed above **D**, the *tonic*, in the bass?

   measure _____

8. Is the final note in "The Giraffe" (**m. 19**)
   the *tonic* or the *dominant*? (circle)
   Circle the most accurate name for the
   chord formed at **m. 19**.

   D   D (add 2)   **D** (add 6)

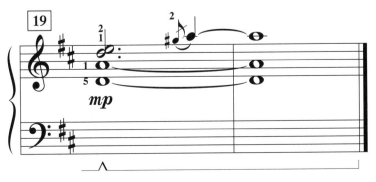

Performance Tip

2-note and **3-note slurs** occur throughout
the piece for an expressive quality (see **mm. 3-4**).

Gently *drop* into the first note. Use the wrist to
roll forward through the slur for a softer last note.

长颈鹿
The Giraffe

Composed by Li Yinghai

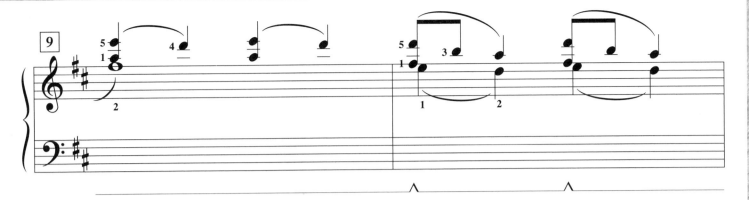

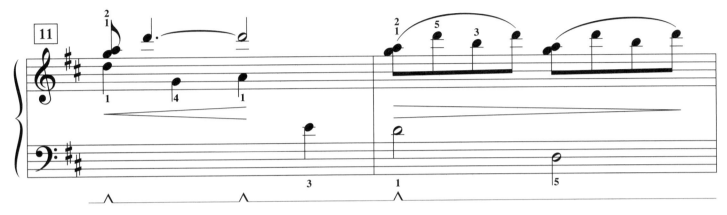

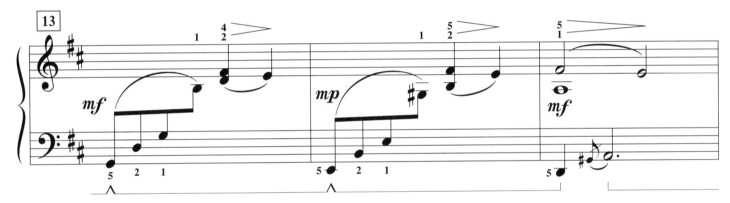

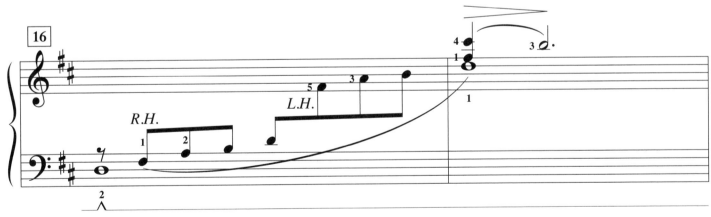

12

Introduction to *The Peacock* (pp. 14-15)

The third piece in the suite, "The Peacock," is a graceful waltz-like dance in B♭ major. The "peacock dance" originated from the Dai ethnic minority. The Dai are famous for their singing and dancing. The peacock dance is one of their most popular dances.

The dance imitates the peacock's gestures and movements based on its daily life. It includes these colorful characteristics: a peacock launching into flight, strutting about, searching for water, and spreading and shaking its magnificent wings.

Think Theory: *The Peacock* (pp. 14-15)

1. Name the **key** for "The Peacock." _____
   Does it begin on the *tonic* or *dominant*?

   _____

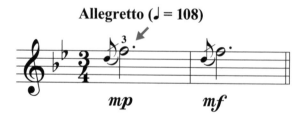

Allegretto (♩ = 108)

2. Play and *memorize* the **two-octave B♭ major scale,** hands separately.
   Note: Circled notes indicate *flat* keys. The highlighted finger numbers will help you see **scale patterns**.

Two-Octave B♭ Major Scale: for R.H.

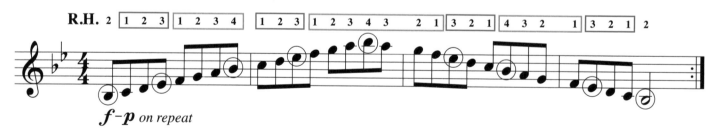

f-*p* on repeat

Two-Octave B♭ Major Scale: for L.H.

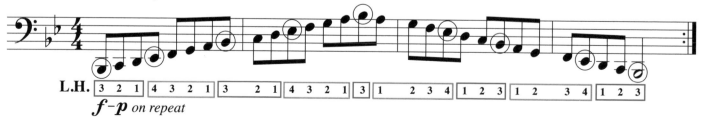

f-*p* on repeat

3. A **triad** (3-note chord composed of 3rds) can be built on each tone of the major scale.
   Triads **I**, **IV**, and **V** are **major chords** and use upper case Roman numerals.
   Triads **ii**, **iii**, and **vi** are **minor chords** and use lower case Roman numerals.

Play and
learn:

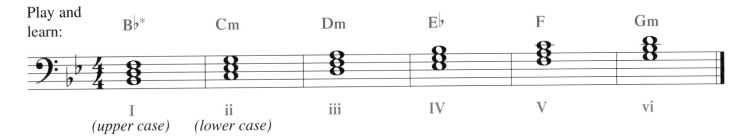

	Bb*	Cm	Dm	Eb	F	Gm
	I	ii	iii	IV	V	vi

(upper case)   (lower case)

4. Circle the correct **chord letter name** shown *above* each example.
   Circle the correct **Roman numeral** shown *below* each example.

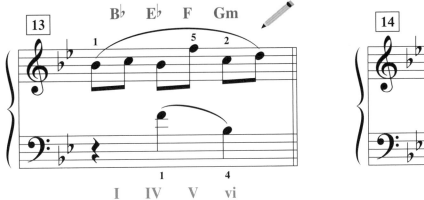

Bb   Eb   F   Gm

13

I   IV   V   vi

Bb   Eb   F   Gm

14

I   IV   V   vi

Bb   Eb   F   Gm

16

I   IV   V   vi

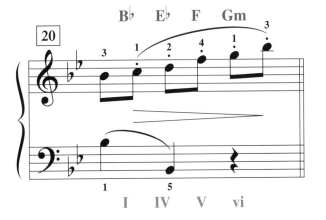

Bb   Eb   F   Gm

20

I   IV   V   vi

5. Look at the ending for
   "The Peacock" (**mm. 26-28**).
   Why is it technically a good
   idea to use the **L.H. finger 3**
   on the final *tonic* note?

26

p

pp

* A capital letter denotes **major** (Ex. Bb).
   A capital letter and lower case "m" denotes **minor** (Ex. Cm).

Performance Tip

- Use a light *wrist bounce* for the **5ths** in **mm. 4**, **6**, and **10**.

孔雀
The Peacock

Composed by Li Yinghai

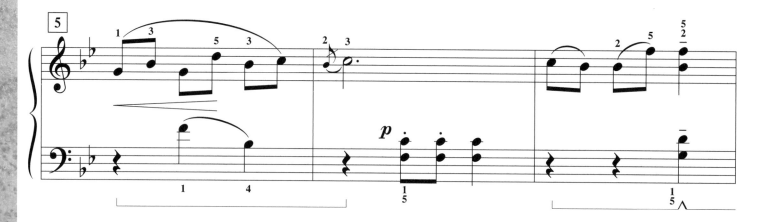

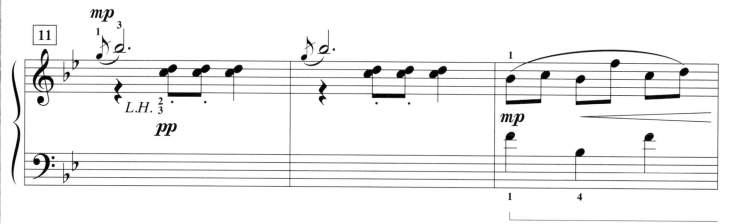

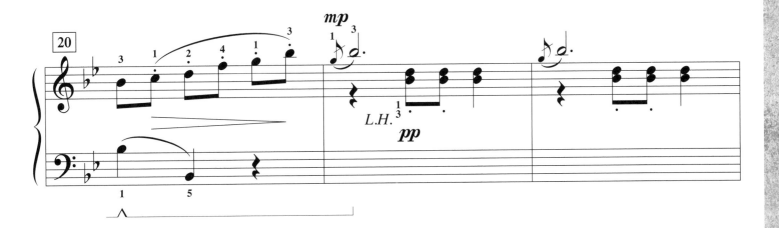

Think Theory: *The Little Monkey* (p. 17)

1. Look at **p. 17**. Name the **key signature**. _____ **major** or **minor** (circle one) ✎

2. Play and *memorize* the **two-octave E♭ major scale**, hands separately.
   Note: Circled notes indicate *flat* keys. The highlighted finger numbers will help you see **scale patterns**.

   Two-Octave E♭ Major Scale: for R.H.

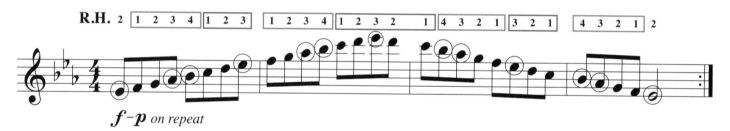

   Two-Octave E♭ Major Scale: for L.H.

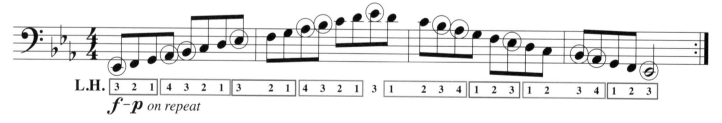

3. What **interval** defines the playful *staccato* opening? _____ (see **p. 17**)

4. In **mm. 5-6** the L.H. and R.H. "outline" a **C minor 7th** chord: C—E♭—G—B♭

   This harmony extends through **m.** _____.

5. Where does the **Cm7** broken chord return at the end of the piece? **Mm.** _____ and _____

6. In **mm. 14-15** the R.H. and L.H. present an **F minor 7th** chord: F—A♭—C—E♭

   This harmony extends through **m.** _____.

Performance Tip

- **Technique hints** are shown in blue throughout the piece.

小猴儿
The Little Monkey

Composed by Li Yinghai

One quick gesture!

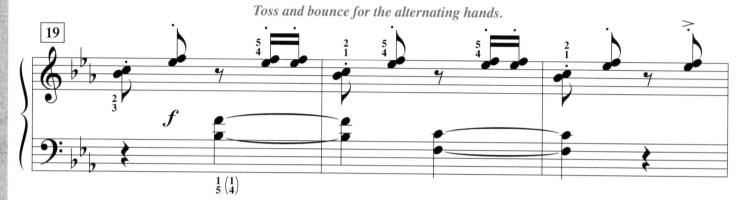

Toss and bounce for the alternating hands.

One quick gesture!

Quick gesture!

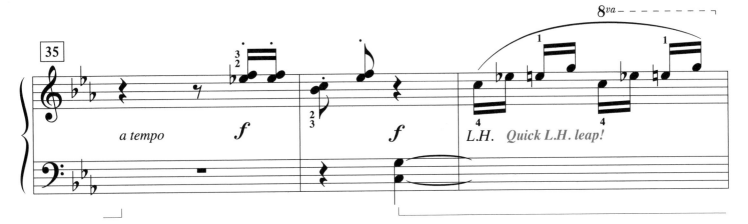

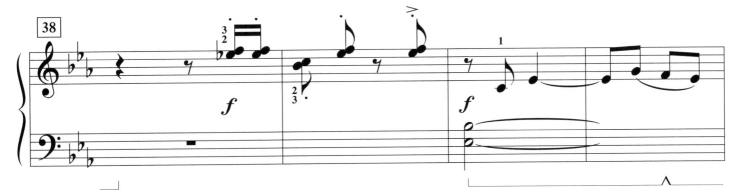

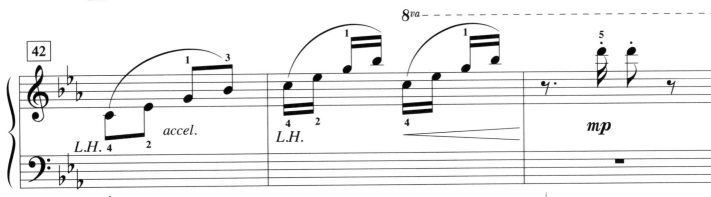

Introduction to *Dragon Lantern Dance* (pp. 20-21)

The dragon lantern dance is a favorite event at the Lantern Festival, a Chinese Holiday celebrated 15 days after the Chinese New Year. Its history dates back over 2,000 years! In the dance, a dramatic, colorful dragon is supported by poles held by dancers. The dragon is guided to do all kinds of interesting movements—dancing, kneeling, leaning, shaking, twisting, and waving. The dragon dance is a symbol of good luck and prosperity.

THE SOUND OF A DRAGON LANTERN DANCE

"Dragon Lantern Dance" has a strong, percussive opening! (**pp. 22-23**)

1. Notice the L.H. open **5th** from **G-D**.

2. The **A** in the accented R.H. chord forms a **2nd** and **4th** for a dramatic sound. Play, feeling the accent on beat 2.

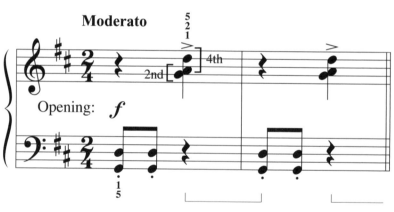

3. The melody is based on the **D pentatonic scale**. First, play the D pentatonic scale. Notice the *skip* (3rd) from **F♯—A**.

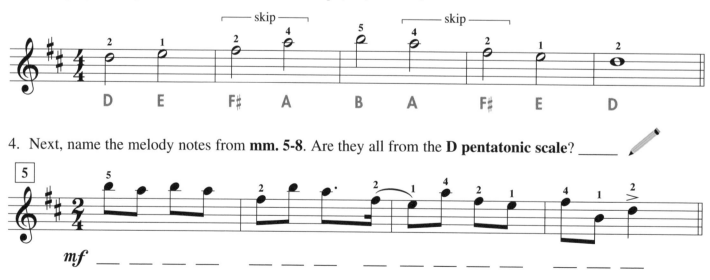

D   E   F♯   A   B   A   F♯   E   D

4. Next, name the melody notes from **mm. 5-8**. Are they all from the **D pentatonic scale**? _____

5. Play the **D pentatonic melody** above. What note dips below the *tonic* **D**? _____

CREATING A DRAGON LANTERN DANCE

Let's expand the **D pentatonic scale** by bringing **F♯-A-B** *below* the **D**. Play until it's easy!

Duet Improvisation Activity

- Your teacher will play a duet based on "Dragon Lantern Dance" (**pp. 22-23**).
  Listen to the **tempo** and **mood**.

- When you are ready, create your *own* sounds using the **D pentatonic scale** shown above.
  Play the notes *in any order*. Here are some ideas to explore:

  — Play **2nds**, **4ths**, and **5ths** based on the scale tones.

  — Try some short **16th-note** patterns.

  — Explore repeated notes, *staccatos*, and accented tones.

- End on any **D**.

Teacher Duet: (Student plays HIGHER on the keyboard)

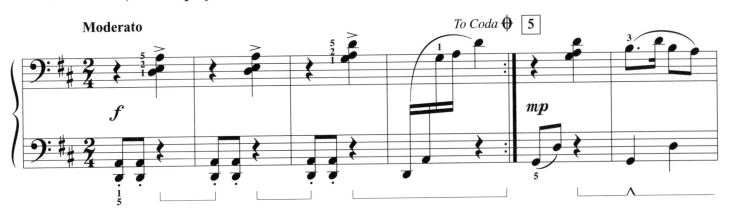

22

Performance Tip

- Emphasize the accent on **beat 2**.
  This helps give a strong, proud sound.

舞龙灯
Dragon Lantern Dance

Composed by Li Feilan

Notice how the pedal marks help accentuate the second beat.

Harmony Alert!

In **mm. 13-16**, the tonality outlines **A major**, the *dominant*.
Does the harmony return to **D**, the *tonic*, in **m. 17**? _____
Where does the music go to the *dominant* again? _____
Does the piece end on **D**, the *tonic*? _____

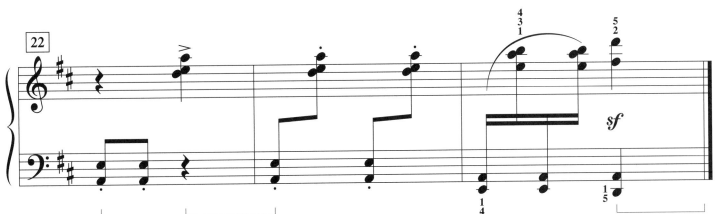

Introduction to *Shepherd's Song*

Shepherd songs are common in China, reflecting the peacefulness of gazing at large pastures.

This piece is built on a **two-hand gesture** that never ceases for the entire composition. The *alternating* meters $\frac{5}{8}$ to $\frac{6}{8}$ unify the piece rhythmically, setting up a lilting flow.

Performance Tip

- Study the markings in the music to help you recognize the *rhythm patterns*.

牧童的歌
Shepherd's Song

Composed by Li Chongguang

OPENING SECTION

Flowing gently

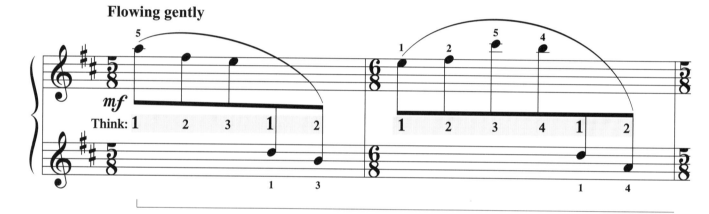

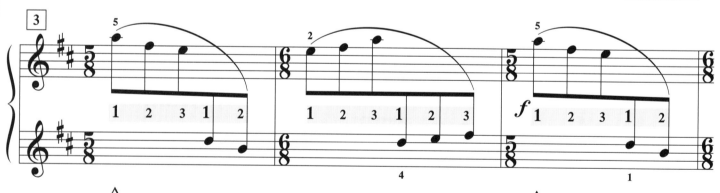

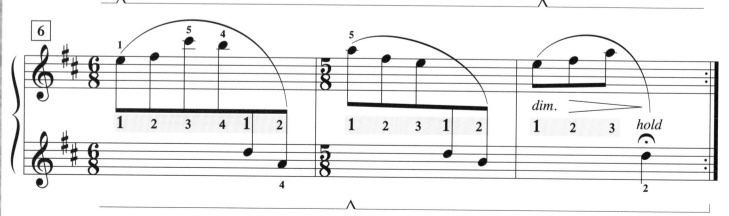

TRANSITION PASSAGE

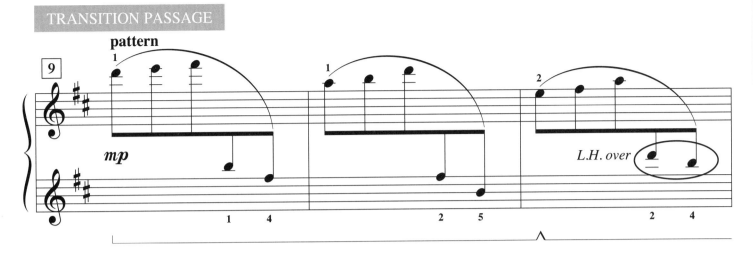

Measures **13-20** are the *same* as
measures **1-8**, transposed down a 5th.

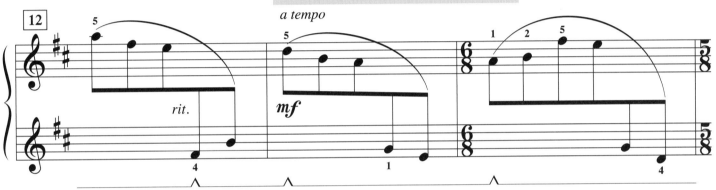

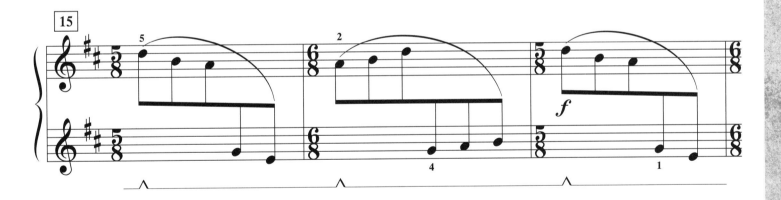

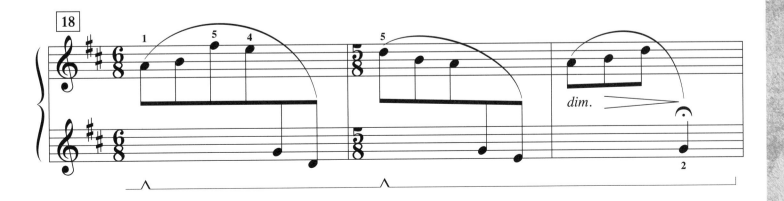

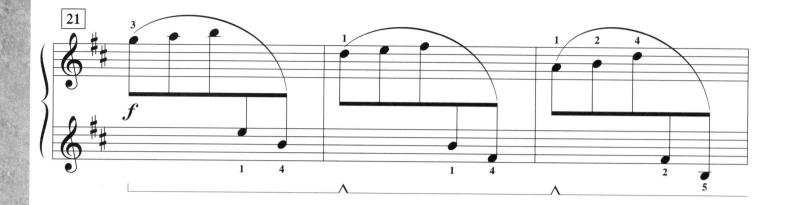

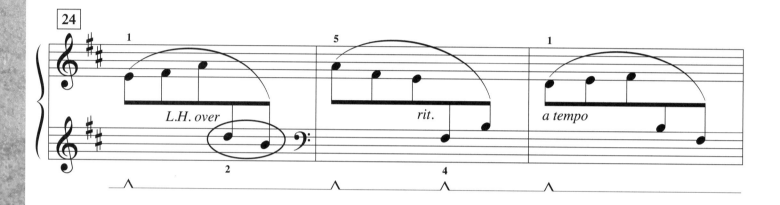

RETURN OF THE OPENING SECTION

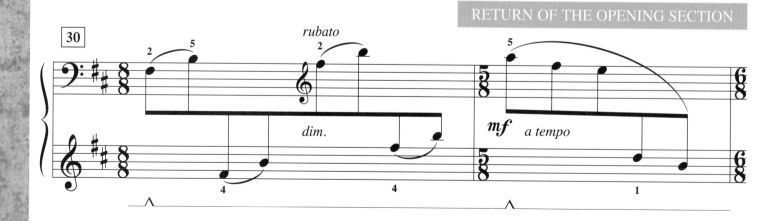

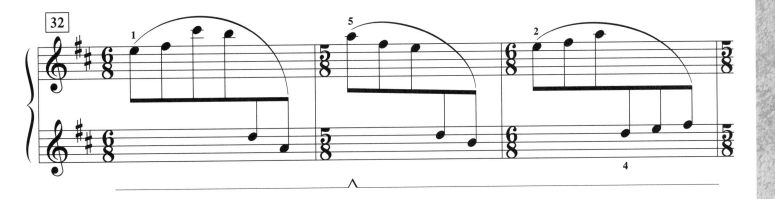

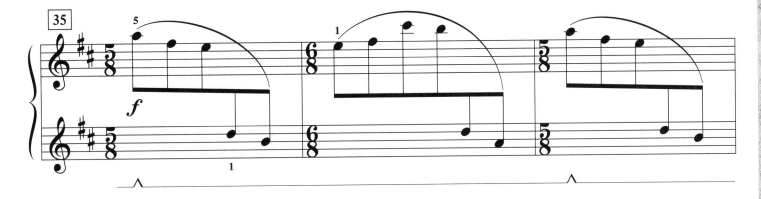

The ending repeats **mm. 9-12**.

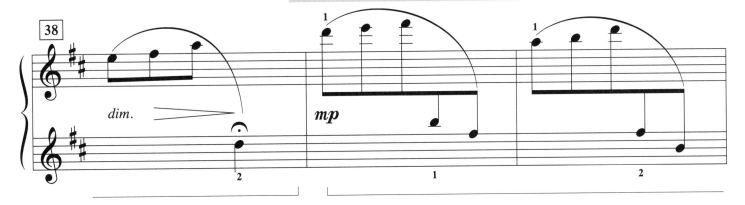

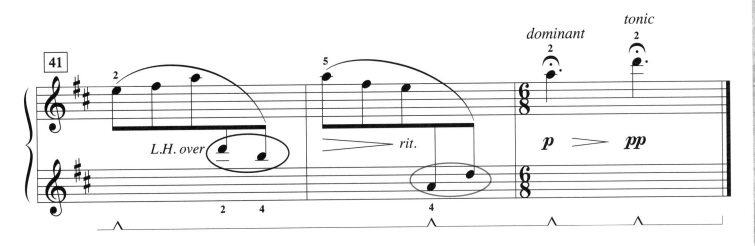

27

This energetic piece is based on the **G major chord** but with *color tones* (notes outside the harmony giving musical interest).

Performance Tips

1. The **L.H. C♯** in the *Alberti bass* creates a quirky effect. Give a slight stress on the downbeat.

2. At **m. 5**, the **R.H. B♭** to **B** creates a humorous shift between major and minor. Choose the fingering you find easiest.

3. At **m. 4** and **m. 12**, short **chromatic** passages give a mischievous effect. Keep your fingers close to the keys.

4. Remember to **practice s-l-o-w-l-y** for control. Being as playful as a "monkey on a bike" requires skill!

小猴骑车
Little Monkey on a Bicycle

Composed by Li Feilan

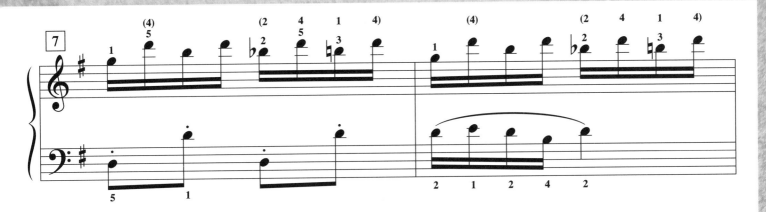

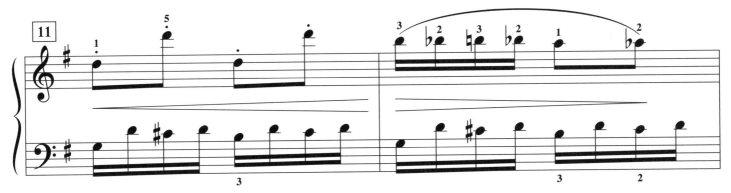

Think Theory: *Hide and Seek* (pp. 31-35)

1. Look at **p. 31**. Name the **key signature**. _____ **major** or **minor** (circle)

2. Play and *memorize* the **two-octave A major scale**, hands separately.
   Note: Circled notes indicate *sharp* keys. The highlighted finger numbers will help you see **scale patterns**.

Two-Octave A Major Scale: for R.H.

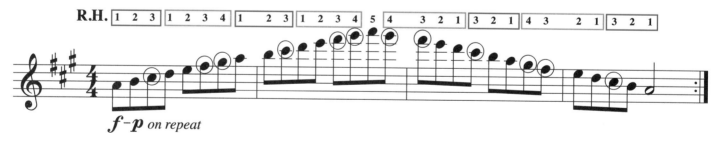

Two-Octave A Major Scale: for L.H.

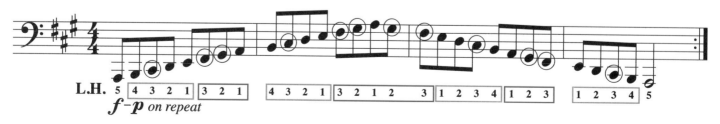

Performance Tips

1. The tempo mark **scherzando** (*tempo rubato*) means playfully with a "give and take" of the tempo.

2. Maintain a comfortable, steady beat to set up the **rubato** passages to come.

3. Circle the *accelerando* (*accel.*) and *ritardando* (*rit.*) marks to alert you to moments of rubato.

捉迷藏
Hide and Seek

Composed by Ding Shande

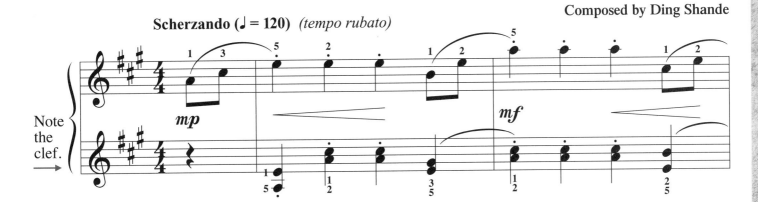

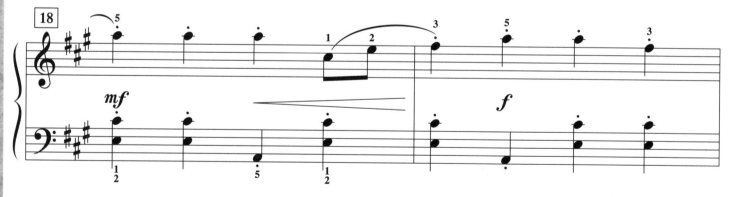

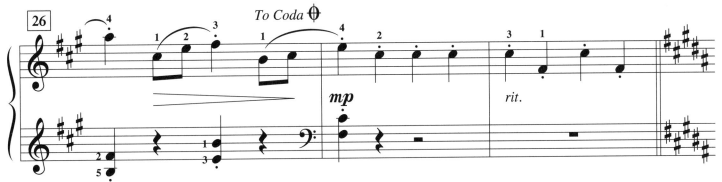

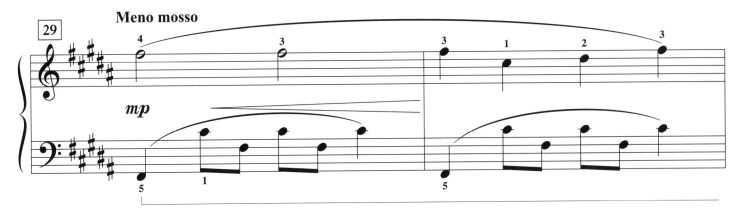

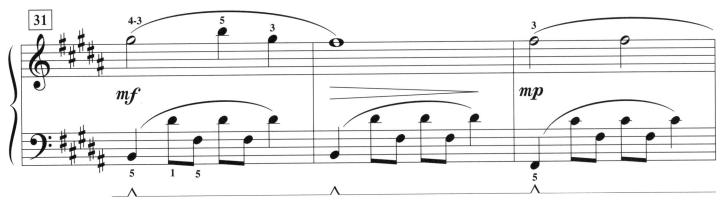

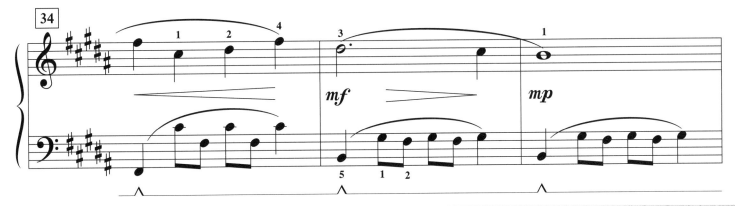

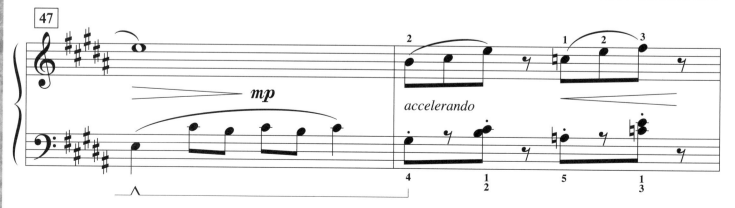

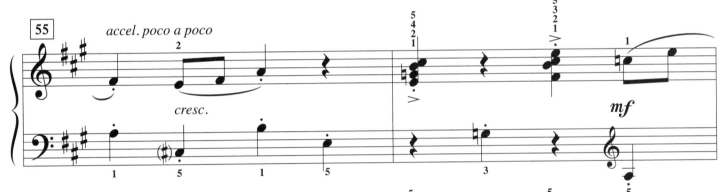

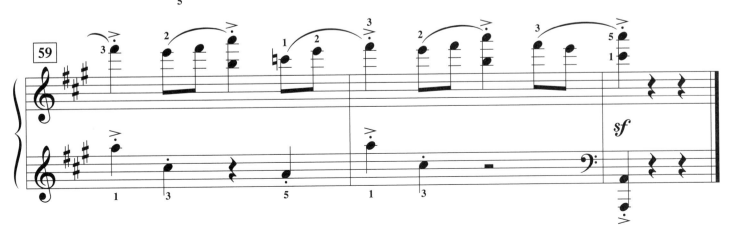

The Composer Is You!

In this book, "The Peacock," (**pp. 12-15**) is a waltz-like dance built on the **B♭ pentatonic scale**.

Follow these steps to compose your *own* piece using the **B♭ pentatonic scale**.

- Use the two **accompaniment patterns** shown below. Play each several times.

Pattern 1   **Pattern 2**

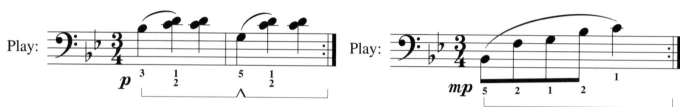

- Next, play the **B♭ pentatonic scale** several times until it's easy. Follow the **fingering** and notice where the *skips* occur.

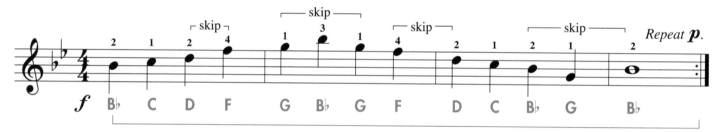

- Now, create a melody using notes from the **B♭ pentatonic scale**. Use the sample rhythm given in blue or create your own.

_____

Title

_____

Composer (your name)

Allegretto

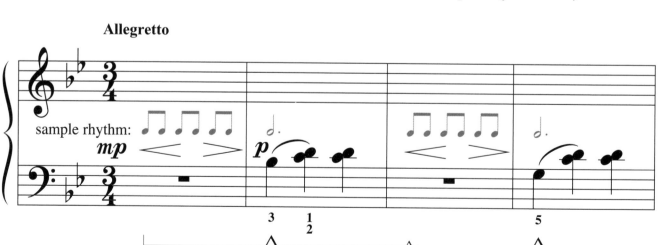

sample rhythm:

For the *Coda*, consider repeating **m. 17** and fading. Or, create a new pattern
for each measure that climbs high up the piano. It's all up to you!

DICTIONARY PUZZLE

Use terms from the **Music Dictionary** (p. 40)
to complete the puzzle.

ACROSS

1.   Walking speed.

2.   Gradually increase the tempo.

7.   Depress the damper pedal.

8.   A five-note scale common in
       Chinese music.

10.   Return to the beginning and play to the
       sign and then jump to the *Coda* (ending).

12.   Expressive quickening or slowing of the
       tempo without altering the overall tempo.

13.   Hold the note its full value.

16.   A sudden pronounced accent.

19. *ff* Very loud.

20.   Little by little.

22.   Moderately.

24.   An ornamental note played quickly
       into the note that follows.

25.   Less motion; slower.

27.   Rather fast, cheerful.

28.   Return to the original tempo.

DOWN

3. ◁ Play gradually louder.

4. 𝄂 Ending section.

5. ▷ Play gradually softer.

6. Rather fast, but not as fast as *allegro*.

9. 8*va* Play one octave higher (or lower) than written.

11. Play this note louder.

12. *rit.* Gradually slowing down.

14. Slowly, but quicker than *largo*.

15. 𝄵 Two half note beats per measure.

17. Abbreviation for *fortissimo*.

18. *p* Soft.

19. ⌒ Hold this note longer than usual.

21. In a playful manner.

23. A little faster than *andante*.

26. Abbreviation for *mezzo-forte*.

29. Abbreviation for *mezzo-piano*.

30. *f* Loud.

MUSIC DICTIONARY

pp	*p*	*mp*	*mf*	*f*	*ff*
pianissimo	*piano*	*mezzo-piano*	*mezzo-forte*	*forte*	*fortissimo*
very soft	soft	medium soft	medium loud	loud	very loud

crescendo (cresc.)
Play gradually louder.

diminuendo (dim.) or *decrescendo (decresc.)*
Play gradually softer.

SIGN	TERM	DEFINITION
⋗	**accent**	Play this note louder.
	accidental	A sharp or flat note not in the key signature. A natural is also an accidental.
	allegretto	Rather fast, but not as fast as *allegro*.
	allegro	Rather fast, cheerful.
	andante	Walking speed.
	andantino	A little faster than *andante*.
	a tempo	Return to the original tempo (speed).
	cantabile	Singing melody.
⊕	**coda**	Ending section.
¢	**cut time**	$\frac{2}{2}$ time. 2 half note beats per measure. A ♩ (instead of a ♪) gets the beat.
	D.C. al Coda	Return to the beginning and play to the sign and then jump to the Coda (ending).
	fermata	Hold this note longer than usual.
	grace note	An ornamental note that is played quickly into the note that follows.
	largetto	Slower, but quicker than *largo*.
	meno mosso	Less motion; slower.
	moderato	Medium speed.
	motive	A short musical idea.
8va – ¬	*ottava*	Play one octave higher than written. When 8va – ⌐ is below the staff, play one octave lower.
‿∧‿	**pedal change**	Lift the damper pedal as the note (or chord) is played. Depress the pedal immediately after.
⌊___⌋	**pedal mark**	Depress the damper pedal after the note or chord.
	pentatonic scale	A 5-note scale common in Chinese music.
	poco a poco	Little by little.
rit.	*ritardando (ritard.)*	Gradually slow down.
	rubato	An expressive give and take of the tempo.
	scherzando	In a playful manner.
	sforzando	A sudden, pronounced accent.
⋍	**tenuto**	Hold this note its full value. Hint: Press deeply into the key.
	theme and variations	A musical form which starts with a theme which is then altered or "varied" through any given number of variations.
	theme	The main melody of a composition. (Many works have more than one theme.)